HOME IS WHERE THE HEART GOES

A MOVING AWAY
BOOK FOR KIDS

XT AND ILLUSTRATIONS
CHLOE E. GORE

This cute little girl with a cheerful smile and happy eyes is Mia.

She loves playing in her garden and feeding the birds.

a enjoys listening
their happy songs
d spending time
tdoors.

One sunny Sunday, as Mia picks flowers in her garden, her parents call her inside with an excited tone.

Mia skips inside, her flowers in hand, and asks, "What's the big news, Mommy and Daddy?"

Her parents smile and say, "We have a surprise for you, Mia! We're going to move to a new house in a different town!"

Mia's wide eyes reflect a whirlpool of emotions.

She has never moved before. The word "new" feels like a grey cloud covering her sunny world.

"But Mom," Mia stammers, "What about my friends? And my school? And our big, beautiful tree in the backyard?"

Mom pulls Mia into a warm embrace, "I understand, sweetheart. Change can be scary. But remember, we'll still have each other.

And just think about all the new friends you'll make and new things you'll learn."

Yet, Mia remains full of worry. Her dad, seeing her distressed, kneels down to her level and says, **"You're braver than you think.**

o you remember the first day of
:hool?"

Mia nods, recalling the memory.

he was terrified, but it turned out
o be one of her favorite days.

And how about when you first rode
our bike without training wheels?"

he remembers, a shaky start but she didn't fall.

nstead, she felt free and proud.

That's right!" Dad says, a proud glint in his eyes, "Just like
hose times, this move might feel scary at first, but I believe
ou'll find amazing things in our new place."

After a moment's thought,
Mia asks, "A new house? Will
there be a garden like this
one?"

Her parents nod. "Yes, darling.

We'll have a new garden, new
friends, and lots of new
adventures!"

Mia's heart feels a little heavy at the thought of leaving her familiar surroundings behind, but she realizes that change can also bring new and exciting things.

So she packs her favorite toys and says goodbye to the garden, promising her favorite tree that she will visit it again someday.

As moving day arrives, Mia watches her room slowly empty of toys and clothes. Her garden is left behind, and she waves goodbye to her favorite tree once more, saying, **"See you soon, Mr. Tree!"**

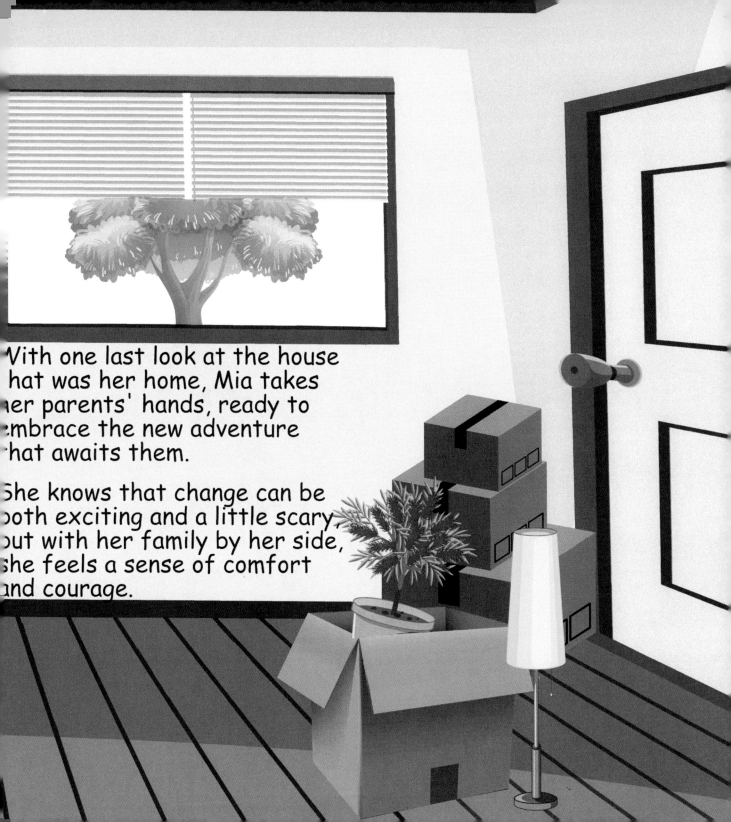

With one last look at the house that was her home, Mia takes her parents' hands, ready to embrace the new adventure that awaits them.

She knows that change can be both exciting and a little scary, but with her family by her side, she feels a sense of comfort and courage.

In the car, Mia's heart is filled with mixed emotions: excitement for the unknown and a tinge of sadness for what she is leaving behind.

She whispers to herself:

"Here we go, Mia. New adventures await!"

When they arrive at their new house, Mia looks out the window with big eyes.

The house is painted in a bright and happy yellow color.

Mia thought the house would feel really nice, but when she sees it, she realizes it's not exactly how she imagined.

The girl peeks out the window and says, **"Oh, the house is yellow! But it's not what I expected."**

Her heart feels a little sad.

Her first days in her new home are difficult. She misses her old friends and feels a little shy before meeting new ones.

"Mom, I miss my old friends. Will I meet new ones?" she asks often.

Mom reassures her, "I understand, sweetie. Change can be hard. But it's also an opportunity to meet new friends and create wonderful memories."

"Why don't we go to the park? There are children playing there. You might make new friends," she suggests.

Mia's heart fills with hope and excitement as she imagines herself joining the children in their joyful play. She nods eagerly, ready for this new adventure.

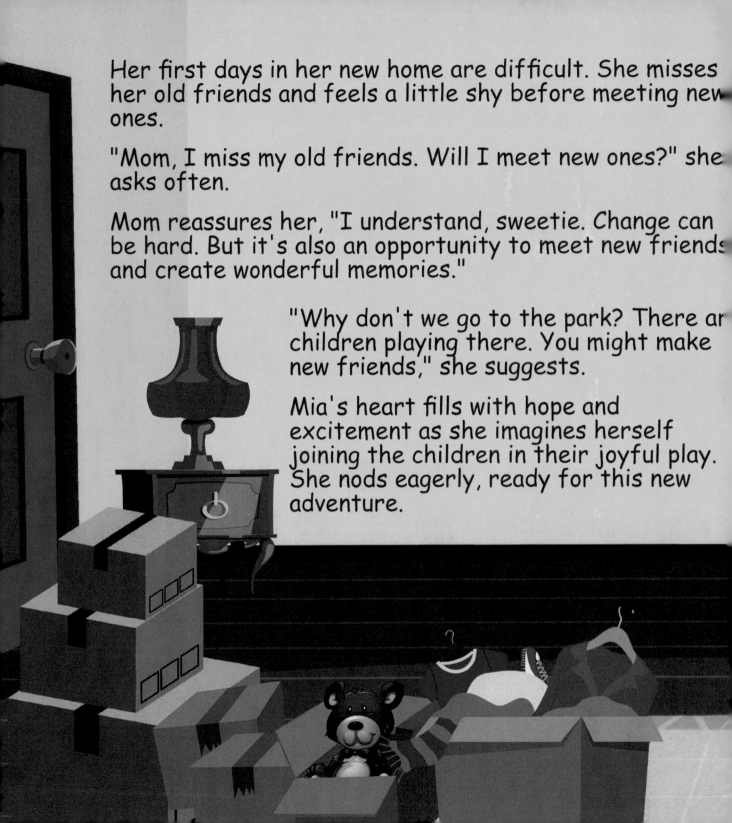

Mia and her mom make their way to the park, hand in hand. As they approach, the girl sees children running, laughing, and playing together. Her heart races with both nervousness and excitement.

"Mom, what if they don't want to play with me?"

Mom gives Mia a reassuring smile,"Don't worry, sweetheart. Just be yourself, and I'm sure you'll make new friends in no time. Remember, everyone here is looking to have fun too!"

The girl takes a deep breath, gathering her courage. She walks closer to the children, her stuffed bunny, Hopsy, still tightly clutched in her hand.

"Hi, can I join you all?" she asks.

The children turn to her, **"Of course! We're playing tag. Come join us!"**

Mia's face fills with happiness as she joins the game.

She runs and plays with her new friends, feeling at home: **"This is great fun! I'm glad I came to the park."**

Mom looks at her with pride from afar. She knows that Mia's bravery has allowed her to make new friends and have fun.

As the sun starts to set, Mia realizes that Hopsy, her beloved stuffed bunny, is missing. She looks everywhere but can't find him.

Mia feels a little sad because Hopsy was special to her.

Mom comes over and gives her a comforting hug,"Don't worry. Sometimes things go on their own adventures. Let's believe that Hopsy will find someone who needs him just as much as you did."

Mia doesn't want to go back to the new house without her bunny. She was very attached to him and he reminded her of their old house.

"Mom, I can't come back home without Hopsy. He's my best friend from our old house."

Mom understands her daughter's love for the toy, but explains that sometimes we have to let things go.

. Together they can find a way to bring a little bit of the old house to the new one.

Mia still feels sadness, but slowly begins to understand mom's words. She knows that memories are eternal, even if things change.

"It's okay, Mom. Maybe when we get home, I'll put Hopsy's picture on the cabinet in my new room."

Mom smiles, proud of her daughter's strength, "That's a great idea. We can also make new memories and find new friends in our new home. And who knows, maybe we'll find something just as special as Hopsy."

"I'll try. But I'll always love Hopsy and remember our old home," Mia replies.

With Mom's support, she is moving toward a new home. Although it's not easy, she knows that change can bring new adventures and happy times, even if she still misses her old place.

As the days turn into weeks, Mia's new home becomes more and more familiar.

Her room fills with laughter and fun, and the garden blooms with colorful flowers.

She spends her free time together with her new friends.

In the meantime, her old home becomes a treasured memory that is fondly remembered, but she doesn't miss it so much anymore.

One evening, Mia looks up at her mom,

Mom, I think I understand now. Home isn't just a house, or a place.

t's where ve plant our oots, make friends, and create memories. It's where love grows. Right?"

Her mom hugs her tightly, tears welling in her eyes. "Yes, my brave girl. Home is where the heart is."

Mia understands that she holds her old house in her heart, in the memories she has, the lessons she has learned, the love she has given and received.

And while she looks forward to new adventures, she knows that home is not just a physical place, but first and foremost a family.

Made in the USA
Las Vegas, NV
24 January 2024